BOUGHT WISDOM is an amazing resource for educators and administrators and students from any discipline, and for those who value teaching and learning. The stories, lessons, and anecdotes that Dr. Burks shares in BOUGHT WISDOM will forever resonate within you.

> **SANDI MCCREE, MFA,** *actress (Delonda Brice in HBO's "The Wire" and Bobby Brown's mother, Carole, in BET's "The New Edition Story"), youth advocate,* and *president, Thought Provoking Arts Company*

I have found him to be an authentic care-taker, passionate advocate, and keenly intellectual educator who balances both theory and practice in such a way as to provide an achievable but forward-thinking and provocative vision.

> **DARIAN C. JONES, PH.D.,** *K-12 education expert* and *founder and chief academic officer, Sankore' Prep*

You walk in his shoes, feeling the awakening pinch of failure and the joy of triumph.

> **KADHIR V. RAJAGOPAL, ED.D.,** *author, Create Success! Unlocking the Potential of Urban Students*

more . . .

[BOUGHT WISDOM is] an inspirational read for all ages containing valuable spiritual nuggets embedded within each story. [It is a] wonderful example of living life with strength, courage, and a sense of adventure!

REV. SHARON THOMPSON, co-spiritual director, Living Truth 365

[Dr. Burks] is insightful and painfully honest about what it takes to get [organizations] and professionals to perform at high levels as well as the tremendous amount of sacrifice involved.

STANTON E. LAWRENCE, SR., ED.D., assistant superintendent for administration, San Antonio Independent School District

[Dr. Burks] is one of the young geniuses engaged in the noble work of transforming K-12 Education and is a leader who knows the value of "learning without limits."

RONNIE PRICE, vice president of human resources, Chattahoochee Technical College

Tony's writing is engaging, delightful, and thought-provoking.

RUBY K. PAYNE, PH.D., author, A Framework for Understanding Poverty and Learning Structures

more . . .

BOUGHT WISDOM warms the heart, tickles the funny-bone and kindly asks its readers to playfully ponder and then participate.

> **FRED-RICK L. ROUNDTREE, MFA,** *special assistant to the provost, Winston-Salem State University*

His work exemplifies culturally courageous leadership in every respect, causing me to feature him in a chapter of my book … He really walks his talk.

> **JOHN ROBERT BROWNE II, ED.D.,** *author, Walking the Equity Talk: A Guide for Culturally Courageous Leadership in School Communities* and *CEO, Third Millennium Enterprises*

BOUGHT WISDOM creates conditions for leaders to become their own best teachers.

> **LARRY D. COBLE, ED.D.,** *co-author, The Hidden Leader* and *Staying on Track*

Tony Lamair Burks II is a passionate educator and a strong advocate for students. He is an impressive role model for lifelong learning and self-improvement with high achievement aspirations.

> **LIBIA GIL, PH.D.,** *assistant deputy secretary and director, Office for English Language Acquisition, United States Department of Education*

ALSO BY THE AUTHOR

The Tale of Imani the Bunny

The Journey to Authenticity: 8 Secrets to Getting the Life You Desire by Mitchell L. Jones (with Tony Lamair Burks II)

Leave with Love: A Spiritual Guide to Succession Planning and Transitions for Charismatic Church Founders by Rev. Dr. Barbara Lewis King (with Tony Lamair Burks II)

To Angela and Wendell for opening your home and your hearts to me and others! TB

BOUGHT
WISDOM

Tales of Living and Learning

TONY LAMAIR BURKS II

LEADright

Atlanta, Georgia

Earlier versions of some chapters in this book appeared in the following publications:

> "On Becoming" in the Carolina Peacemaker
> "My First Teacher" in the Carolina Peacemaker
> "Tie Bow" in the Williamson A.M.
> "A Place at the Table" in *The Principal Reader: Narratives of Experience*
> "Going the Extra Mile" in *Rules of the Game: How to Win a Job in Educational Leadership: Insider Tips and Trade Secrets to Help you Score Your Goal*
> "Truth be Told" in the Carolina Peacemaker

Cover Photo by Marie Thomas www.mariethomas.com
Cover Design by Nuri Abdur-Rauf www.nuriabdurrauf.com
Copyediting by Richard Allen bytewise1815@gmail.com

Printed and bound in the United States of America

Bought Wisdom: Tales of Living and Learning, Volume I / Tony Lamair Burks II — 1st ed.
ISBN 978-0-692-87118-8

DEDICATION

I dedicate this book to my grandparents—Mary Etta Matthews Potter, Lillie Mae Carter Smith Burks, Monroe Lee Potter, and the Reverend Timothy M. Burks—to my mentors—Rupert Hickman, Selden X. Bailey, the Rev. Dr. James A. Smith, Franklin Jones, Bonnie Dickens, Sterling H. Hudson III, Dr. John Fitzgerald Gates, Richard O'Hara, David Mallery, Eugene Howard Wade, Dr. Terry B. Grier, Dr. Preston McKever-Floyd, Dr. John Robert Browne II, Dr. Randolph E. Ward, and Dr. Joseph F. Johnson Jr.—to my students—from California, Tennessee, North Carolina, Georgia, and abroad—to my protégés—especially Luqman, Mona, Chaz, Marshall, Aquannette, Taijuan, and Carl—to my teachers and professors—especially the Rev. Joyce Whiting, Josephine Glanton, Paulette Clardy, Minnie West, Evander Vann Burkett II, Dr. Marcellus Chandler Barksdale, Dr. Melvin B. Rahming, Dr. Joceyln Jackson, the Rev. Dr. Aaron L. Parker, Dr. Aníbal A. Bueno, and Benjamin P. McLaurin—to my brothers from other mothers—Anthony Tyrone Bostic, Dr. Rodney L. Boone, Piaget Todd Averyhart, Dr. Harley F. Etienne, Morgan Scott Tucker, Christopher Lamont Jolley, Marc Fields, Effren Joseph Villanueva, Avery Carson, Willie Lateef Neil, Timothy Daniels Knight, Winston Warrior, Terence Deon Dillard, Ronnie Charles Banyard, Jr., Jason B. Allen, Bishop David Earl Jackson, Dr. Roderick Dwayne Ford, Mitchell L. Jones, Tolton Ramal Pace, Steven Christopher Anglin, Dr. Will Carroll, Stephen Gregory Barr, Trover K. Reeves, and the distinguished gentlemen of Alpha Phi Alpha Fraternity, Incorporated—to my sisters from other misters—Yakima Simone Rhinehart, Valerie Dawn Bouldin, Angel P. McCurdy, Kelly Reneé Nance, Chantel

Deneice Mullen, Esq., Tonya Winters Buford, Deborah Smith—to my Thanksgiving Crew, both old and new—to the ECG A-Team—Valerie Dawn Bouldin, Larry "Guy" Ferguson, Lisa Boyles Kiser, and Dr. Kathrynn Adams—to the Senior Associates at LEADright for support—to the Pubsters at the Center for Responsive Schools—thank you for your dedication to publishing thoughtful works that save lives—to colleagues from Guilford County Schools, especially Alan Jerome Hooker, Sharon Ozment, and the GCS Doctoral Cohort—to Great Schools Partnership for walking the equity talk—to my classmates at the Barbara King School of Ministry—Kim, Ife, Jada, William, Chantell, Bryan, Millicent, Edward, Jeremy, Andrea, Jocelyn, Rebecca, and Gloria—to the Dothan High School Class of 1989 and the Morehouse College Class of 1993 for friendship—to my wellness team for keeping me aware, fit, and flexible for the challenges of this life—Dr. Patrick Coleman, Antawn Morris, Harvey Maclin, Leah Neaderthal, Anthony Nelson, Rev. Priestess Calister, Dr. Christopher Holmes, and Karla Mays—to Alexa, Justin, and Amir for teaching me how to be a parent—to my extended and interconnected family— Burks, Potter, Eddings, Kelley, Carter, Smith, Matthews, Bostic, Boone, DeShazor, and Chapman—to Hillside International Truth Center and Living Truth 365 for supporting me in living my truth daily—to my sugarplum for love unconditional—and to my many "other mothers" and mentors—the Honorable Rose Evans Gordon, Caroline Grace Blackwell, Elder Marjorie Johnson Ward, Dr. Shirley Morrison, Lucille G. Smith, Addie Bell Anglin, Willie Lee Thomas, the Rev. Dr. Diane L. Givens Moffett, Peggi Crawford James, Margaret Flakes, Dr. Donna Y. Ford, Dr. Anne Wimbush Watts, Dr. Barbara Zwadyk, Mildred Phillips, Dr. Angela Bass, Dr. Grenita Lathan, Brenda Joyce Daniel, the Rev. Dr. Joan Speaks, the Rev. Sharon Thompson, Bishop Yvette Flunder, and Bishop Barbara Lewis King—who lift me and whose stories encourage me to fly.

Sometimes people give you grief because they don't know your story, but you know you couldn't help anybody if you didn't have a story. The reason that you are such a blessing is because you have a story and you ought to spend more time telling your story because you can set a whole lot of people free with your story. Don't be afraid to tell your story because it's some truth that's gonna make us free. Tell your story and see if God don't promote you!

January 1, 2017

Rev. Dr. Yvette A. Flunder
Founder and Senior Pastor
City of Refuge United Church of Christ

Presiding Bishop
The Fellowship of Affirming Ministries

Author
Where the Edge Gathers:
A Theology of Homiletic Radical Inclusion

Permission to use granted February 13, 2017

CONTENTS

ACKNOWLEDGMENTS

Books—of any genre, of any length—owe their existence to a cadre of encouragers and supporters: seen and unseen, sung and unsung.

Thank you to Lora Maxine Hodges, Ed.D. for sharing hard-earned, bought wisdom and inspiring the title of this work.

Thank you to Principal Mitzi Yates Lizàrraga for inviting me to speak to the graduating seniors at her school, the San Diego School of Creative and Performing Arts. That speech was a seed that grew into this work.

Thank you to Rebecca Gay Adams, Ph.D., Anthony Tyrone Bostic, Valerie Dawn Bouldin, John Robert Browne II, Thomas Kirk DeShazor Jr., and Wanda Hill Legrand, Ed.D. for reading the original manuscript and for offering pieces of stories that I'd shared with them over the years, yet somehow had slipped my mind as I was writing.

Thank you to one of my mentors, the ever-living David Mallery, a consultant to independent schools who provided funding for me to attend "Writing Our Lives: A Seminar for People Who Write (or who would like to write)." David's thoughtful critique of "On Becoming" transformed the essay into a noble work—and, in the process, it transformed me.

Master Storyteller Donald Doyle, Ph.D. offered a summer workshop in 1999 at the Tennessee Arts Academy. I was blessed to be one of his students. When pressed for a story to share on the spot, I told the story of Preachin' John Grubbs. Don coached me on telling the story with feeling, rhythm, and passion. The final version appears in this book.

Thank you to Sharon Thompson, Larry D. Coble, Kadhir V. Rajagopal, Ruby K. Payne, Fred-Rick L. Roundtree, and Sandi McCree for reviewing an advanced copy of this book and offering praise.

Thank you to Richard Allen for his copyediting and proofreading prowess. He formatted my dissertation in 2008 and in the years since, I have heard scores of newly-minted doctors rave about his gifts. This work—much like my dissertation—is better because of him.

To the thief who stole my backpack in Barcelona, Spain on my 45th birthday (i.e., December 28, 2015) minutes before the cruise ship left the port, thank you. You took more than my 6-month old laptop and three external hard drives, you absconded from the bus with the only hard copy of this book along with four years of handwritten edits and feedback. Nothing is ever lost in Spirit and what was to be included in *Bought Wisdom* came back to me with photographic clarity.

Actor and writer Thandiwe and educator LaKenji encouraged me to welcome other stories I'd locked out of my memory: stories of rejection, betrayal, and pain. They pushed me to include these stories to "flesh out" the full human experience. For this I am grateful.

I am appreciative of Sylvia High, Deborah Smith, Mike Mercedes, Moira Taylor, Elona Jones Shelton, Kym Kennedy, and the Aiming High Leadership Team Eight (aka LT8/LTB) for standing with me and supporting me in completing the final version of this manuscript.

I am indebted to Charles Philip Gause, Ph.D. and Doris Potter Hickman for coaxing another book from within me: first, my dissertation, and now, *Bought Wisdom*.

To my step-parents—Tori L. Adams and the ever-living James "Duke" Culver—thank you for loving me deeply and unconditionally as your son.

To my parents—Janice Elaine Burks and Tony Lamair Burks—who have loved me since I was but a twinkle in their eyes: I am honored to be your only child. This book is also for you.

FOREWORD

I remember the first time I met Tony Lamair Burks II. It was at the opening reception for the 2002 school year at The Early College at Guilford. We parents of incoming students had waited for this day since our children had applied for admission by the April 15 deadline that spring. We were a risk-taking bunch; we had allowed our children to accept admission to a school that had no principal, no teachers, no classrooms, and no textbooks.

Nonetheless, even risk-takers have their limitations when their children are involved, and we were anxious to meet the man who was going to guide them through the next few years. Would he be up to the challenge? Was he a kindred adventurous and creative spirit or just another bureaucrat trying to move up the career ladder?

In *Bought Wisdom*, Tony quotes an Asian saying: "May you live in interesting times." My own father often paraphrased that same saying when he was commenting on what he and my mother had learned from raising my brother, sister, and me, but he called it a curse: "May you have interesting children."

If having interesting children is a curse, Tony was one of the most cursed men I knew that fall, because our children—his students—were certainly interesting. We parents worried that this new principal would not understand them well enough to nurture them. On top of everything else, hardly anyone in Greensboro was in favor of the establishment of the school—not the School Board who thought public school money should not be wasted on bright students, not the principals of other high schools who resented the departure of some of their most promising students, and neither the faculty nor students at Guilford College who thought the high school students would lower the quality of education. This principal had to be special because he was going to have a heck of a job in front of him. Fortunately, he was and is special. Actually I tell people that thanks to Tony's vision and leadership my daughter, for all practical purposes, managed "to escape high school."

I don't remember everything about the reception that first day of my now ongoing friendship with Tony, but I do remember a story he told, or at least the moral of the story (yes, he tells stories with morals all of the time; it is not just hype to rationalize this book). It was a story about how some colleagues had been reprimanded by a former supervisor for letting her go all day with sweet potato on her face without telling her. He said he didn't want to have to find out that he had sweet potato on his face at the end of the day; he wanted to be told as soon as we noticed. Then he invited questions and expressions of concern. So began an open dialogue about what the school would be and who, as a result, our children would be.

This invitation to discuss these topics convinced me to become active in the parent-student-teacher organization, which I had previously avoided in other schools my daughter attended because of what I perceived to be prejudice against working mothers. Much to my pleasant surprise, the parents were as interesting as their children and many of them were as old as my husband and I were (our daughter was born when we were in our mid-thirties). As the secretary of the organization, I served with a former corporate executive, a CPA, a lawyer, and other professionals. Tony inspired us all to help with the school by asking us to use our professional skills for the collective good. In so doing, he acquired a dedicated unpaid "staff" before he had hired enough teachers to cover classes.

Tony inspired everyone to be a part of the team, including the students. He told the students, "You want a club, start one." And they did. He told the students, "You want sports, start one." And they did. He told the students, "You want a disciplinary code, write one." And they did. "You want a dance, plan one." And they did. And he told us all, "You want a school? Call it a 'school' and not a 'program,' and, by the way, go to relevant School Board meetings if you want them to continue funding it as well." And we did, parents and students alike. And so forth and so forth.

I do not mean to imply that all Tony did was delegate, because he was there for every single one of us, students and parents alike, inspiring us, guiding us, and helping us grow. He still knows what each one of his "shining stars" from The Early College is doing. They all know they can call him about anything, anytime, and they do still call him. It is a habit they developed as students when Tony gave them all his cell phone number and told them he was available 24/7. I suspect they were are motivated to call him because every single day they were in high school he gave them a new opportunity "to refuse to accept someone else's definition of who" they were, and because they knew he would help them "buy some wisdom" from whatever challenge or success they were facing. By sharing his own successes and challenges, Tony made students feel comfortable sharing their own aspirations and concerns before opportunities had passed or crises had emerged.

So Tony did rise to the challenge of establishing The Early College at Guilford and nurturing our students. Although placing the first two classes of students in college was challenging because the school was unknown, Tony did not rest until each one of my daughter's college-going classmates had been accepted at his or her first-choice college. He called admissions departments, wrote to them, and advocated for each and every one of our students. Today the name "The Early College at Guilford" speaks for itself. The Phoenix that Tony used to brand The Early College has indeed risen. Reading *Bought Wisdom* and responding to the questions Tony poses after each story gives others the opportunity to learn from Tony's stories and "from experiencing life and all it tosses your way."

Rebecca G. Adams, Ph.D.
University of North Carolina at Greensboro
Greensboro, North Carolina

FOREWORD

I relocated to Greensboro, North Carolina in 2002 to establish one of the first early college high schools in the nation. Imagine arriving at a high school with no textbooks, no computers, nothing. No mission or philosophy, no traditions or heritage, nothing. Such was the case when we opened The Early College at Guilford that fall. Two teaching positions were vacant and many of our textbooks were trapped on a delivery truck a few weeks before students were to arrive. Computers were stolen from the school's main office just hours before the first day of school. And what's more, we didn't have a single student club, a school mascot, a school song, or school colors.

It's been well over a decade since we gave birth to a school that has been replicated across the continental United States and beyond. We've

grown a little older—and hopefully a little wiser—
since we first huddled around a red-draped table at
Elizabeth's Pizza in hopes of creating something
transformative. I'm thankful for the strong bonds I
maintain with colleagues from Guilford College,
our host institution, and with the faculty, staff, and
alumni of The Early College at Guilford. I am
equally thankful for lasting friendships that have
survived job changes, relocations, marriages,
breakups, and setbacks.

Believe it or not, all of this brings me to Lora
Hodges. It was Dr. Hodges who first told me the
real definition of the educational term AYP. "AYP
doesn't mean 'Adequate Yearly Progress,'" she
quipped, "AYP means 'Ain't You the Principal?'"
It was Dr. Hodges who first schooled me on
"Bought Sense." It's the kind of wisdom you get
from experiencing life and all it tosses your way.
It's the kind of wisdom for which you pay a price.
It's loaning $100 to a friend who hasn't paid you
back the first $100 you loaned her two years ago.
It's leaving the house, hearing that still small voice
telling you to go back, and you do so only to find a
loved one on the floor in need. It's knowing whose
Pound Cake you shouldn't eat at the church
cookout. Dr. Hodges says we'd do well to learn
from the "Bought Wisdom" of others.

Badger—a character in one of my favorite books, *Crow and Weasel* by Barry Lopez—talks about the importance of storytelling. She says,

> *The stories people tell have a way of taking care of them. If stories come to you, care for them. And learn to give them away where they are needed. Sometimes a person needs a story more than food to stay alive. That is why we put these stories into each other's memory.*

I hope these stories—my "Bought Wisdom"—will find a place in your memory. I hope my "Bought Wisdom" will inspire you to write your own stories so you may "give them away [when and] where they are needed."

Tony Lamair Burks II, Ed.D.
Atlanta, Georgia

A WORD ABOUT YOUR REFLECTIONS

You'll find space to journal at the end of each story. Although I offer a few questions and prompts to "prime the pump" and get your journaling juices flowing, I invite you to journal in a way that makes sense to you. Feel free to doodle, sketch, or write as you question and reflect. A friend and fellow educator, the ever-living Judy Butler, shared this on her website years before her death:

> *I hope this website gives you ideas for including journaling in your classroom in whatever form may inspire your students. . . . I am a learner who has always found it easier to draw than to write, to doodle while listening, and to make the concept visual to help me understand it. You may have children in your class right now who work the same way. Give them the chance to express their ideas in the way that is best for them. This may not always be the way that is best for the standardized test—but in third grade and now at age 62 it is the way that cleared my path of discovery. http://judybutler.com/home.htm[1]*

May you discover more about yourself along the way.

---

[1] The website is no longer active. Permission was granted by Judy Butler prior to her death to use this material in *Bought Wisdom: Tales of Living and Learning*. Permission was also sought—and granted—from the family of Judy Butler.

I AM[2]

I am from collard greens and cornbread.
I am from the Heart of Dixie,
the buckle of the Bible Belt.
I am from grits and catfish, bursting with flavor;
cooked with love.

I am from small town America
tutored in the lessons of the past.
I am from chitlins and curry and escargot.
I am from preachers and teachers;
domestics and doctors.

I am from old souls and new beginnings.
I am from the Land of Peanuts, where Cotton was King
and where Carver built a new empire.

I am from tree houses, go carts, plums, and figs.
I am from Corky and Pickaboo; Stevie and Cherokee.
I am from lazy Saturdays spent walking "cross town"
and early Sundays in the Amen Corner.

I am from big city USA equipped to traverse the globe.
I am from Mary and ML, Lillie and Tim,
Janice and Tony.
I am from genesis and revelations . . . what is
and what is to be.

---

[2] Inspired by "Where I'm From" by George Ella Lyon.

ON BECOMING

Some people you never forget. After a few weeks in my first principalship, I unearthed several of my elementary school report cards while unpacking books and artifacts. I was instantly transported to one of my former schools. I saw the face of my grade school principal. Principals were mean, I thought. They were folk who never smiled. They didn't skip. They didn't fly kites. They didn't run or jump. I believed they never had a skipper. They weren't free spirited enough to throw flat rocks into a lake. I secretly believed our principal didn't have a childhood, a home, a life. The last thing I wanted to be was a principal!

Mr. Winstead was my principal. He was knee high to a nickel with a smattering of gray hair. He donned bland suits that swallowed him whole and wore battered brown, lackluster loafers. I despised his shoes. I was appalled his shoes were so ugly. They weren't befitting a man responsible for school

1

peopled with growing children. His shoes must've had stories to tell.

Mr. Winstead didn't take mess from anyone. Not parents, not teachers. Not school board members, and certainly not students. He often resorted to standing behind his desk to create the illusion of authority and power. Somehow it worked. As children, we lived in constant fear of him.

From our perspective, Mr. Winstead never saw us as more than what we were at that time in our lives. We were typical kids who did typical kid things. He didn't like me, or so I thought. Was it my glasses? My scrawny frame? Was he intimidated by my briefcase? (Yes, I carried a briefcase from fifth grade until the end of high school.) I'll never know because Mr. Winstead didn't let us get to know him. I never saw him in classes. He didn't speak to us in the hallway. Woe to the student who messed up and had to head to his office. We dreaded that place; he seemed to relish the impact the room had on us. His memory was like that of an elephant. Once you did the misdeed, you could rest assured he'd never forget it.

One day in class, after not feeling challenged in months, I lost myself in witnessing everyday occurrences:

Terry Bryant is mouthing a colorful word or two at Miss Easton. A spider is scaling the radiator. Did he actually say what I think he just said to Miss Easton? I wonder how far away the spider lives? Dang, she swung her paddle at Terry's behind like a Major League Baseball player! Was that spider male or female?

Little did I know that ADHD and giftedness were an undiscovered, challenging mix for a boy-child in Alabama, bored with a stack of worksheets.

Miss Easton, unequipped with the resources to connect with academically gifted students, snatched me from my dubious imaginings and hauled me off to see the principal. I recoiled as Mr. Winstead ushered me down the corridor warning me I'd end up in the Principal's Office for the rest of my life if I didn't shape up!

And I did shape up. Thank goodness for witty, insightful teachers in the upper grades who knew I was not a finished product. Thank goodness for brilliant and engaging college professors who encouraged my transformation. My teachers and professors saw my schoolmates and I not as we were, but as we were becoming. Of course, I've made it to the principal's office countless times since...as the principal!

I didn't know that Mr. Winstead and one of my hometown doctors attended the same church. For over twenty years, my accomplishments were the topic of conversation between the two distinguished parishioners. When this wild child got his first teaching job, Mr. Winstead knew and kept note. He knew of each promotion and stood with pride as I took my first principalship. The man who wore the lackluster loafers I held in such disdain as a child sent regards to me through my doctor when I became principal and magnet school director. My hometown doctor said Mr. Winstead beamed with pride each time, saying, "I knew Tony had it in him all along."

Maybe Mr. Winstead's shoes were weathered because he had spent decades tracking me and other students through all of our transformations, trials, and tribulations. As I think about the graduations, weddings, and promotions of my own students from over my career, I can't help but confess I've been wearing the same battered *Kenneth Cole* loafers from my first principalship—they're almost 20 years old! I appreciate Mr. Winstead and our shoes from a respectful place. Indeed, our shoes have stories to tell.

YOUR REFLECTION

What are you becoming? In what ways have your experiences as a student of life shaped who you are today? Why it is important for us to see each other as more than what we are right now? What do we learn by embracing this way of being?

_____
_____
_____
_____
_____
_____
_____
_____
_____
_____
_____
_____
_____
_____
_____
_____
_____
_____
_____
_____
_____
_____
_____
_____
_____

MY FIRST TEACHER

My mother is like most mothers—she was my first teacher. As such, Mom often shared with me her belief in the power of a solid education. She told me stories of her times in segregated Alabama schools to encourage me. She was the sixth of nine children. They had limited resources, yet their thirst for learning was unlimited.

Although my mother's school may have lacked certain material things under the deeply entrenched system of "Separate but Equal" in Alabama, she and her classmates had a strong web of community support. Segregation gave them a continuous parade of Black professionals as they lived their lives. When Black families needed their teeth fixed, they saw Black dentists. When Black families were ill, they saw Black physicians. When Black families needed legal help, they saw Black attorneys. Segregation required my mom and her family to turn to the Black community for their needs.

My mom dreamt of a world where I would live beyond the madness of our American brand of "-isms." She dreamt of a world where restrictions based on gender or race or age would not hinder me if she could determine my path. The world she dreamt is the world she created for me.

My mother created her own school choice program for me. She would research each elementary school. Then she chose which school would best suit me at each grade level. My mother exposed me to the most effective educators she could assemble. She knew I had one shot at excellence and she didn't have the time to waste waiting on schools leaders to coach and train ineffective staff to excellence.

By the time I entered middle school, I had attended four elementary schools. Michael C. Patton was my principal for grades four and five; Mr. Patton had also been my mother's teacher. She knew I would flourish in a school led by him. His values and those of my mother were aligned toward excellence. When Mr. Patton retired, he had served my hometown school district forty years as an educator!

My mother insisted I get mentors and challenged me to learn from them. Selden X. Bailey strode into the Hawk-Houston Boys Club one afternoon and decided he'd be my mentor. He was a decisive man. He'd served with the Third Emergency Rescue Squadron of the United States Army Air Forces during World War II eventually rising to the rank of Colonel. I didn't know his military service or anything else about Mr. Bailey when we meet other than his son, Chip, was a football player-turned politician.

Mr. Bailey had a mission and he approached his service as my mentor with dedication and tenacity. He gave me solid advice about my zany childhood entrepreneurial pursuits. And he was persistent about me going to college. "Now, Tony," he'd often say, "It's either the University of Alabama or Auburn University." College was never "if" or "when" with him. It was solidly "where." Mr. Bailey and I were a seemingly odd mentor-protégé couple. An elderly white guy and a young black boy, Mr. Bailey and I periodically joined his dear friend Eustace E. Bishop, Sr. for hot dogs and conversations about politics, philosophy, business, and life. Whether I was selling candy, making holiday wreaths, or running for superintendent of my hometown school district, Mr. Bailey invested in my growth and advocated for me.

My mother's expectations of me were higher than any standardized test would ever be. She nurtured my creativity and individuality. She encouraged me to "buckle down" and be "ten times better" than the rest. She supported my educational travels to Greece, Mexico, Egypt, and Japan. She'd help me raise money and raise awareness about my work in education. Also, she reminded me that my academic performance must always be rooted in compassion and integrity.

I know my mother's love for me is not unlike the love other mothers have for their children. I'm grateful because she backed this love with action. Once my mom connected with my schooling at Miss Lottie C.'s Daycare, she remained linked until I walked across the campus green of Morehouse College to receive my diploma. This was challenging work for her because she worked the ever-changing schedule of a telephone operator and supervisor. Amazingly, my mom met with my teachers for 19 out of the 25 years I was a student.

Even at Morehouse, professors and administrators knew my mom for her candor and involvement. She developed a friendship with one administrator, Benjamin P. McLaurin. Mr. McLaurin headed the College's Office of Career Counseling and Placement. She would say, "Call me when he's messing up AND call me when he's doing fine." My mom would swing by his office to say, "hello!" Despite her visits to my schools, my mother never became an over-involved, obnoxious overseer or "helicopter parent". I didn't always know of her visits to campus. They were short, uneventful status checks. She inspected what she expected.

In retrospect, I guess the only thing that kept my mother from getting involved during my doctoral studies at the University of North Carolina-Greensboro was the eight-hour driving distance! Whatever the case, I give thanks for her gift of presence.

YOUR REFLECTION

Think about the family "you made" (e.g., your circle of friends who are not related to you by "blood"). Also, think about the family "that made you" (e.g., your parents and any siblings). How were they involved in your growth and development? What roles did they play in your formal and informal education? What lessons did they teach you through their words and actions (or inaction)? In what ways are you like them?

_____

_____

_____

_____

_____

_____

_____

_____

_____

_____

_____

_____

_____

_____

_____

_____

_____

_____

_____

_____

TIE BOW

I was the quiet kid who wielded a briefcase and sported wire-framed glasses. My huge glasses were a wall, shielding me from others. My briefcase was my security blanket, comforting me with a symbol my peers found unapproachable. All of this changed when I met a distinguished gentleman named Rutherford Whitmore III.

Mr. Whitmore was an arresting sight. I happened upon him as he ambled down the street as confident as any mogul. His navy double-breasted blazer was tailor-made. His slacks were creased to a razor-sharp perfection. His monogrammed cuff links were weighty and ornate, but not gaudy. His crisp dress shirt was a pristine canvas upon which he presented a masterpiece: his bow tie. This was not just any bow tie—it was a hand-tied bow tie.

"Clip on bow ties," he bellowed, "are for little boys."

I was drawn to his bow tie as much for its purple hue as for the sheer mystery of how he tied it together. That evening I rushed out and bought my first bow tie. The salesperson at the store taught me how to tie it. It was a beauty, a silken blend of earth tones and paisleys to be worn on special occasions. And I had just the event in mind!

My high school was abuzz with excitement surrounding commencement. All of us—even the jocks—were giddy as we rehearsed the program. Our senior advisors ran down a laundry list of what we couldn't wear for the ceremony. Girls were to wear pant suits or collarless dresses. Guys could don slacks, although a coat and tie were preferred. Jeans, shorts, and sandals were definite no-nos. The senior advisors were tough. Of course, they didn't mention bow ties, so I decided to wear my new bow tie to our baccalaureate service—religious service honoring the graduating class—on Sunday.

That following Sunday we paraded into the Civic Center before thousands of family and friends. Just as I was about to stroll down the aisle, a senior advisor commanded I tuck my bow tie inside my gown. I was appalled; yet, I complied with her demand. Six days later at graduation I put on my bow tie and was again told to tuck it in. "What must I do?" I thought about what the bow tie meant to me as I sat with my classmates. My bow tie—tied slightly askew—demanded attention and respect. I was alive when I wore it. Each time I did so, I became that dapper gentleman who shared with me his love for bow ties.

I stood up when the marshal arrived at our row, and exhaled. I knew what had to be done. Then as that magical moment approached, I liberated my bow tie and crossed the stage to receive my diploma. I kicked aside the notion of respectability and conformity. I would not adapt or readjust my spirit to make "The Powers That Be" happy. They were livid. But what could they do? I had just graduated.

And what began as a small act of rebellion for a country boy has become a trademark accessory. I wear my bow tie as a symbol of individuality and freedom. I wear it as a reminder of my commitment to service.

YOUR REFLECTION

American journalist Warren St. John notes that "[W]earing a bow tie is a way of expressing an aggressive lack of concern for what other people think." Have you experienced daring to be different? If so, what did you do? How did the experience shape you? What might you do differently were you to experience a similar situation again? What did you gain from being authentically you?

EXPERIENCE REQUIRED

When I graduated from high school in 1989, I was so ready to leave my hometown. I'd gotten a few unsolicited partial and full scholarships from a handful of in-state colleges and universities. However, when my mentor, Selden Bailey, simply asked, "War Eagle or Roll Tide?" I responded, "Morehouse College!" "Now that's a great choice, Tony. That's Dr. King's alma mater." Four short years later I graduated from Morehouse wondering, "What's next?" Sterling Hudson, another mentor, encouraged me to consider teaching. He felt it was a great match; after all, I'd spent every summer in Atlanta working with the Morehouse-Spelman Early College Summer Program. I took Dean Hudson's advice and sent letters of interest to dozens of independent schools across the nation.

At first, there was silence. Then, letters trickled in. And then came the flood; I stopped counting after receiving thirty rejection letters. I grew accustomed to reading all kinds of comments: "Sorry, no philosophy positions." And my favorite: "Contact us once you get some experience." Experience? How would I ever get experience if no one would give me a chance?

In late June of 1993 I received a call from The Branson School in Ross, California about serving as a teaching intern. They wanted to give me a chance and I became the school's first Bess K. Gallard Teaching Fellow. Bess Gallard was before her time. As a teacher in the Los Angeles Unified School District, she embraced diversity before it was in vogue. I was told she saw the color of each student and celebrated her students for their cultural and ethnic giftedness. I was told her teaching was culturally responsive long before the concept was popularized. Her son-in-law, Robert Haas, who was Chair and CEO of Levi Strauss at the time, endowed the fellowship in honor of her and her deep commitment to equity and diversity.

Leaving the comfort of my beloved South expanded my worldview in ways I couldn't have imagined. Branson was an eye-opening experience. I discovered a love for the environment when I visited nearby Muir Woods. I expanded my palate with a mélange of foods from around the world. I was thousands of miles away from home; I had time on my hands, so I reflected on my life. I had time to ask all sorts of questions: "Why must I teach?"; "What are my gifts?"; "What else do I want to do?" It was really the first time that I was with people from such diverse backgrounds. Diversity in Alabama was reduced to black folk and white folk. In California I found an ethnically diverse population of white, black, brown, yellow, and red people. I met people who were gay, straight, and transgender, each comfortable being uniquely themselves. It was also my first taste of socioeconomic diversity. Branson is in Marin County, one of the wealthiest counties in the nation. I can say that I learned more about socioeconomics in that one year than I had learned during the previous twenty-two years. I learned that people of the same race or ethnicity could be galaxies apart in their thinking; class and wealth were the distinctions.

The highlight of my experience in California was teaching history courses with John Roosevelt Boettiger, a master teacher and the grandson of Franklin Delano Roosevelt. John was an engaging teacher who thoughtfully guided me through my fellowship. He advocated foregoing the prolonged observation time period and instead plunging into teaching headfirst. He also built strong connections with his ninth-grade students by facilitating rich classroom conversations. My Branson experience was a time of learning on the fly and pioneering the fellowship. It was my first-time teaching so I had to learn many things, including course content days—if not hours—before the students did. I devoted part of that year to branding the fellowship. I refused to use the title "intern" when I communicated on campus. I believed having a teaching fellowship meant that I surely must be the teaching fellow.

At the end of the fellowship, I was faced with a dilemma: remain at Branson in a non-teaching role in hopes of filling an opening in a couple of years, or search for a teaching position elsewhere. With Dr. Boettiger's encouragement, I decided to cast my net wider and pursue a full-time teaching position. The rest is history!

YOUR REFLECTION

Describe a time when you encountered rejection. What did you learn about yourself from the experience? How did the rejection shape you and your journey? There are times when we must get out of our own way—our comfort zones—to bravely go into uncharted territory. How are you facing a situation that will require you to leave your comfort zone? What lessons are you learning? How might you help others learn from your experience?

TRAILBLAZING

I never thought I would move to Tennessee, especially to Nashville; however, the University School of Nashville (USN) hired me as a philosophy and history teacher in 1994 and I packed my car and loaded a moving truck bound for the Deep South. USN was a welcoming place: It was the most diverse independent school in the state with people from varied experiences and backgrounds. I taught all kinds of classes, chaperoned annual grade-level retreats, and visited Egypt twice. I led kids around the United States and Jamaica to do community service, and I spent a month in Japan. I began to see myself in many ways as a catalyst. I had a blast at USN, a place that once was the demonstration school for the George Peabody College for Teachers. My goal was to awaken that same spirit, that same yearning I felt during my time at Morehouse College within my students. I grew tremendously as a teacher during my almost five-year stint at USN. I was involved with the school's professional organization, I'd stuff staff mailboxes with educational and inspirational readings, I worked with others to get a diverse menu of professional development opportunities, and I prepared food for people on a whim just to say "We appreciate you." I grew so much that I was embarrassed by some of the things I had done as a teaching fellow in California. I remember teaching a unit about a particular group of people in early civilizations. At the start of a new unit, I pronounced the group's name one way and a student whose father was from the region kindly corrected me and pronounced it another way. Despite her cultural linkage to the people and place, I assured her my pronunciation was the correct version. We continued the lesson and months later I discovered I was wrong. Not only was I embarrassed by my mispronunciation, I was humiliated by my stubborn determination to be correct. Somehow, I'd learned that the teacher had to be right all the time. This was untrue and unhealthy; USN helped me dismantle this madness brick by brick. It was a place of learning and I was content to remain at USN until retirement.

I have so many memories of my time at USN. Perhaps the most pivotal event took place when the principal of USN's middle school announced he would be moving on to a new school (in Hawaii, no less!). This was a marker event for me! "Who would I shadow now?" I was in a total daze; I was shadowing the principal of the middle school for a semester as a part of my graduate studies in educational leadership. The middle school principal asked to speak with me in private and I just knew he was about to tell me to find someone else. Little did I know that he would ask me to strongly consider the middle school principalship—his job! I was flattered, stupefied, frightened, validated, and so much more. I thanked him for holding me in such high esteem. He gave me much to contemplate that afternoon.

When I made it home, I decided to "organize" my administrative portfolio for grad school, which basically meant I would reformat an assignment in the electronic portfolio. This was a way to do something without thinking deeply. It was a nice way to procrastinate, to meditate. I reflected on all that had taken place that afternoon. The current principal told me I had all of the qualities USN was seeking. He highlighted the benefits of my graduate program and its practicum. He even mentioned my race as a factor the school would appreciate. Yeah, lots to digest, lots to think about.

I needed to learn about everything related to the position. I began with feelings, then moved to thinking, then to assessing, and finally to action. I pondered what it would feel like to work as an administrator in a school where I'd been teaching. How would I be treated? Would my friends stop speaking if I walked into the faculty lounge? I wondered what the job of a middle school principal entailed and questioned if I was suited for the work. The feeling was similar to having a sickness, yet being unable to communicate the pain and symptoms to the physician. I knew I was slightly uncomfortable with the position at USN, but I didn't quite know why. Perhaps I was uncomfortable with the prospect of transitioning from teaching to administration. Then I convinced myself this was modesty rearing its head. I thought maybe I was just feeling a little uncomfortable receiving all of this praise. Later on that day a student and a board member asked me if I'd was ready to lead the middle school—I thought I would faint!

I'd been around the school for four years as a teacher, but did I know the expectations of the faculty, the staff, and the upper administration? Was I aware of the board and how it functioned? Had I dealt with the politics of leadership? The more I thought about things, the leerier I became of any prospect of me leading at USN the following year. I emailed one of my educational allies for advice. He told me almost verbatim what I'd heard from professors and read in texts. First, he suggested that I get some mental distance from the school so I could begin the process of gathering important information about the principal of the middle school and his tenure, about community values and traditions, about internal politics that may be at work, and about the true nature of the work he did.

At that point in my life, I didn't think I was where I needed to be to do myself and the school the greatest good. I told him I needed to earn my master's degree first. I wanted more experience doing other things at the school. I didn't want to be "that" kind of trailblazer—"USN's first black principal!" I didn't want the pressure. I'd found that black educators who worked in predominantly white schools often told stories of intense scrutiny—degrees and credentials judged, and grading practices and academic rigor questioned. The middle school principal was speechless. I told him, "if you could only spend one day as a black person then you would understand the richness of this feeling. I want to lead a school when I feel comfortable with my abilities. I know people will always question my abilities, so it isn't that people will question my competence if I apply for the position. Instead, it's that I'll be questioning it as well, and this would not be good for my overall well-being." In the end, I told the middle school principal, "No thanks." It seemed like it took me forever to get from "feelings" to "action."

Once I said "no" to the middle school principalship, I began to say "yes" to opportunities to stretch myself administratively. That summer I transformed USN's High School Summer Classes Program into The Summer Session at USN, a comprehensive summer experience for students and adults . . . and we made a profit (a first for the program)! Things began to blossom for me.

By choosing to slow down and not rush to take on a position that greatly interested me, I built my capacity as a learner and a leader. I spent more time learning from mentors like Caroline Blackwell and David Mallery who nurtured my passion for leadership. They each gave me opportunities to learn from others. David invited—and at times sponsored—my participation in professional learning experiences like the Westown Seminar on Teaching. Caroline exposed me to diversity, inclusion, and equity by engaging me as a planner and leader with the National Association of Independent Schools People of Color Conference. She also exposed me to tools and protocols to facilitate meaningful learning. Mine was a rich lesson of authenticity, patience, and self-care. I grew personally and professionally, developing and deepening an identity that still informs my life today.

YOUR REFLECTION

Good decision-making sometimes means knowing the limits of your capacity. How have you made yourself aware of your capacity and abilities? How do you continue to learn and grow? What do you do to support others in building capacity and abilities? How do you "grow" people? Think of a time when you decided you wouldn't do something. How did that decision impact you? How did you evolve?

QUEEN MOTHER OF DANCE

We were lucky. Actually, we were blessed.
There we were rolling along Interstate 70 East,
heading back to Tennessee. We'd completed
another successful Alternative Spring Break (ASB)
trip. Months before we made our way to East Saint
Louis, Illinois, my students at the University School
of Nashville raised money to sustain us for the
week-long service learning experience. As one of a
handful of chaperones, I drove, facilitated
reflections, and joined in the work of serving the
chosen community. All of us—students and
teachers alike—gladly pitched in when it came to
preparing meals.

We had much to consider on our return trip.
Things had gone as planned—well, at least for the
first few days. I don't recall why East Saint Louis
was chosen, but we'd partnered with a community
agency to provide people-power to renovate a
couple of homes in one of the communities. Some

of us installed roofing shingles. Others painted walls and hung siding. Some of us removed rubbish. Others organized interiors. We were a mightily efficient band of volunteers, so much so that we ran out of volunteer work to do in a few days.

Since we had more Spring Break left than we had service learning projects, we checked in with community organizers for more options. Some of us were dispatched to a fledgling farmers' market to spruce things up. Others went to homes and churches in the community helping get things together for a community-wide yard sale. I helped with yard sale preparations. I am my mother's child. An item caught my eye; I quickly purchased the newfound treasure to jumpstart their sales. The heirloom chest would be a welcomed addition to my condo once we figured out how we'd get it back to Tennessee! I was so proud of my students for their work ethic and for the collegial and professional manner in which they carried themselves. They were even saying "Yes, sir" and "Yes, ma'am" to those we met. This struck me because these were pleasantries that even my dear, sweet Grandma couldn't persuade me to utter. And, yes, it wasn't long before we'd plowed our way through even more volunteer work.

Someone suggested we collect trash from vacant lots around the neighborhood. This sounded like a great idea, so we swarmed the neighborhood with large black bags, sturdy rakes, healthy (and unhealthy) snacks, and cool water in tow. We happened upon the intersection of Pennsylvania Avenue and North Tenth Street ready for the challenge. We surveyed the area and chose a lot nestled between two stately homes: one was a red brick house, the other was a two-story English Regency townhouse. And there they were: these two architectural jewels in East Saint Louis. We'd done our homework in preparation for our ASB experience; I'd been tutored on the happenings of the area. By all media accounts, East Saint Louis wasn't the place to be after dark. The structures seemed out of place here as much as my white students were in that neighborhood donning their prep school apparel.

We busied ourselves at a steady pace, assured we'd have ample work to do in the vacant lot. After a couple of hours, a woman descended the stairs of the red brick home offering us water and thanking us for our service. She introduced herself, gesturing with the steely grace of a dancer. "Was she a dancer?" I pondered briefly before refocusing on what she was sharing. She informed us that we were standing between the private residence of Katherine Mary Dunham and her Dynamic Museum. My students—for all their intellect—were clueless about the legend. "Who's Katherine Dunham?" one student asked with innocence. My blood boiled as I successfully muffled an acerbic "that's Ms. Dunham to you!" Then as gracefully as she'd entered our presence, the woman was cocooned in Ms. Dunham's residence.

Paralyzed and rooted to the spot, I thought, "Ms. Dunham? Katherine Dunham? The Katherine Dunham!" My mind raced back to 1993 and the Flowers Family. Back then I'd lived on the campus of a local university throughout my year-long stint as a Teaching Fellow at The Branson School. Dr. Parthenia Flowers was a professor of dance at the university. Her daughter, Lia, was one of a handful of African-American students enrolled at Branson. Dr. Flowers took me under her wing, feeding me physically and spiritually. I was welcomed to have a place at her family's dinner table. A Master Teacher, Dr. Flowers had written and lectured about Ms. Dunham. In addition to her professorship, she and other torchbearers led an organization charged with credentialing dance instructors to teach Ms. Dunham's polyrhythmic dance technique. In my twelve months in the Bay

Area I'd come to know a little about Ms. Dunham through the stories told by Dr. Flowers.

And there I was wondering what to do, standing in a field with Ms. Dunham's home a throw of a stone away. I steeled myself and approached the residence. I knocked on the door searching for what to say. The Dancer opened the door with a quizzical look and I asked, "Umm, I don't mean to bother you, but do you know Dr. Parthenia Flowers?" "Parthenia Flowers? Yes, I know Dr. Flowers," she replied matter-of-factly, perhaps wondering where this line of questioning was headed. I told her how I'd come to know Dr. Flowers and her family during my teaching fellowship and how Dr. Flowers had been one of my "Other Mothers." She exclaimed, "You know Theni!?!" as she gave me a quick welcome-to-the-family hug. She disappeared inside again and when she returned, she invited my 12 students and me inside.

As we entered, I drifted off thinking of DeJuan, Juliette, and other dancer-friends who would've given their eye teeth to exchange places with any one of us for the next few hours. I likened Ms. Dunham's home to a living museum of her life as an author, dancer, activist, choreographer, and anthropologist. Images of dancers and tailor-made costumes festooned the walls. I caught a quick glimpse of a 1954 photograph of Ms. Dunham's legs taken by F. S. Schiffer. I learned much later that the back of the image bore two inscriptions:

> *Inscribed in ink*: "Katherine Dunham legs, of which Jean Cocteau said, 'If we writers could say with our pens what Katherine Dunham says with her legs, our writings would be forbidden.'" (Miss Dunham's legs are insured by Lloyds of London for $25,000).
> *Inscribed in pencil*: ". . . for about $1,000,000 by Hurok!"[3]

There were photographs with familiar and unfamiliar faces: Eartha Kitt and Alvin Ailey and John Houston. Sidney Poitier and James Dean and Marlon Brando. Léopold Senghor and Pearl Primus and Shelley Winters. The ascent to the second level where Ms. Dunham awaited was deliberate, permitting my students to absorb the gravity of it all.

Ms. Dunham sat on her bed with the quiet dignity of a monarch. She was dressed in simple

---

[3] Sol Horuk was a 20th century American impresario who managed the careers of notable artists including Marian Anderson and Isaac Stern.

elegance, her frame a fitting display of an assortment of jewelry fashioned from precious and semi-precious stones. She invited us to sit around her—I claimed a spot near the footboard. With the precision and care of a griot—an esteemed storyteller—she talked of her experiences abroad and of the plight of indigenous people. She discussed her 1992 hunger strike prompted by President George H. W. Bush's decision to deny Haitians asylum in the United States. More than anything, she talked of the oneness of humankind and thanked us for doing our part.

We left Ms. Dunham's home enlightened and renewed for the work ahead, but not before we were given a guided tour of the Dunham Dynamic Museum. If Ms. Dunham's home was a living museum, her Dynamic Museum was East Saint Louis's Smithsonian. An impressive collection of symbolic and functional art, the museum included instruments, paintings, sculpture, and other works from over 50 countries. The top floor featured original costumes created expressly for Ms. Dunham by John Pratt, her husband and artistic collaborator for 47 years. A highlight for me was the opportunity to see a few paintings that Ms. Dunham created to "come down" after her engaging and dynamic performances.

Indeed, we had much to consider on our return trip. I began to read all things "Dunham" and I learned so much about her creativity, dignity, strength, and activism. I discovered that she was the first African-American to choreograph for the Metropolitan Opera (it was Aida starring Leontyne Price in the title role). I learned about Southland and her remarks at its premiere:

> *Though I have not smelled the smell of burning flesh and have never seen a black body swaying from a southern tree, I have felt these things in spirit. . . . Through the creative artist comes the need . . . to show this thing to the world, hoping that by exposing the ill, the conscience of the many will protest. . . . This is not all of America, it is not all of the South, but it is a living, present part.*[4]

I learned that hers was America's first self-supporting all-black modern dance group—this was in large part due to her outspokenness about inequality and intolerance. In fact, lesser known and lesser talented dance companies were funded

---

[4] Katherine Dunham, "Southland (1951) A Dramatic Ballet in Two Scenes World Premiere, Santiago de Chile, January, 1951," in M. Needham, ed., I See America Dancing: Selected Readings, 1685–2000 (Chicago, IL: University of Illinois Press, 2002), 217.

and promoted over Ms. Dunham's dance company. She stood valiant in the face of this, continuing to speak out as an artist and as an intellectual.

I learned Ms. Dunham's impact extended beyond her beloved Haiti to Mother Africa. The little-known story is that one day Ms. Dunham discovered that the owner of Club Med had plans to transform Goree Island—with its House of Slaves and Door of No Return—into a resort. The exclusive resort would even ban Africans from gaining membership. Ms. Dunham reached out to the president and religious leaders of Senegal to thwart the plans; the island has since become a UNESCO World Heritage site and a major destination for many African-Americans.

We wouldn't forget our time in Missouri. We couldn't because of serendipity. Somehow we'd found ourselves in East Saint Louis for Alternative Spring Break—out of all of the deserving communities in the nation. Somehow we'd run out of volunteer service work to complete—despite our best efforts to pace ourselves. Somehow we'd found ourselves at the intersection of Pennsylvania and East Tenth (now Katherine Dunham Place)— out of dozens of cross streets in East Saint Louis. Somehow we'd engaged in conversations about things that mattered—despite freedom to discuss whatever. Somehow we'd been invited inside to have an audience with the Queen Mother of Dance—out of all of the people in the world one could meet. Somehow she'd woven all of our conversation points from the stories we'd shared with each other throughout the week into her recollection of a life of service. Serendipity had entered our lives. We were lucky. Actually, we were blessed.

YOUR REFLECTION

Recall a time when you met someone you admired and respected. What do you remember about the meeting? What wisdom did the person share with you? What makes this person admirable and respectable? How does this person influence and inspire others to live their greatness now?

_____

_____

_____

_____

_____

_____

_____

_____

_____

_____

_____

_____

_____

_____

_____

_____

_____

_____

_____

_____

_____

PREACHIN' JOHN

There is an Asian saying that a friend shared with me many years ago: "May you live in interesting times." This saying took on a new meaning for me in 1998. That September and October I'd received several phone calls from a neighboring school district asking me to interview for assistant principal vacancies. I'd lived in Tennessee for almost five years and hadn't heard of the district though it was just minutes south of where I worked. I loved teaching and I knew I didn't want to become an assistant principal at a traditional, comprehensive high school. This was a position I decided I'd never want. By November, however, I figured it wouldn't hurt to interview for the position as practice for future interviews.

I remember it all vividly. After the interview, I was offered a contract on the spot to work as an elementary school principal. As I sat in the conference room with three central office staff members, I did something that blew their minds: I asked the superintendent a few questions. I wanted to know about the two schools where he'd proposed I'd serve as principal. I told the superintendent that it did not make sense for me to choose to go to a school that had had three principals from outside the district in as many years, which would make me the fourth principal in three years.

I'd learned in my short career that the rapid turnover of a line of school principals was a sign of significant problems with culture and leadership. Such turnover required the skill of a veteran leader. Although, I was willing to grow as a leader, I wasn't interested in starting out with attacks from all sides. I then posed other questions. I wished to know how he wanted others to characterize his tenure as superintendent. I wanted to know if I would be working with him or for him.

Even after my frank questions I was given a contract to serve as an elementary school principal. I chose to go to the other school, one in its ninth year of operation that had had one principal since it was founded. In fact, the superintendent wanted me to start December 1, which was less than three weeks away. I was flummoxed, so I called my paternal grandparents and gave them every excuse why I should continue teaching:

> I'd never even been an assistant principal.
> I hadn't taken the state licensing exam.
> The school was 98% white.
> They weren't ready for a 27-year-old Black principal.
> And, they wanted me to start in the middle of the year, less than a month away.

My grandfather—ever wise—reminded me of a story he'd told time and time again. With my divine imagination, I can see him sitting back in his favorite easy chair telling this story now:

> John Grubbs lived on a thriving plantation in the heart of the deep South. Preachin' John, as he was called, had spent his early life enslaved in Georgia. Once he secured his freedom, he became a traveling preacher who believed in the power of dreams. Though Preachin' John loved Georgia dearly, he hated the oppression his people still endured in the state. He knew he had to move elsewhere in order to survive. So Preachin' John thought long and hard, but not

too long and not too hard, and then fashioned a dream.

Around the turn of the century, Preachin' John relocated his family to northern Alabama and built a small, wooden church. His church quickly emerged as a center of community life; he became a teacher and a preacher, unlocking the treasure in each child. In due season, Preachin' John's work began to pose a threat to the ways of the Old South. He was told to shackle his passion for teaching or suffer the wrath of an angry mob.

It wasn't long before what some called "nightriders" and others called "klansmen" threatened to burn his church to the ground. They demanded his life for inciting their sharecroppers to read, write, and rebel. Although Preachin' John loved teaching and preaching dearly, he feared for the lives of his family and his church members. So he thought long and hard, but not too long and not too hard, and then created a plan.

With bags packed, Preachin' John and his family fled for southeastern Alabama. Not long after they resettled, word spread that White men were out to lynch him. While Preachin' John loved travelling dearly, he decided he wouldn't run anymore. So he thought long and hard, but not too long and not too hard, and then changed his name.

You see, Preachin' John Grubbs had merely adopted the last name of a Georgian plantation owner. This was common practice back then. It didn't take much for him to effortlessly slip on a new name to protect his treasured way of life. No one's certain why Preachin' John chose his new family name; all that is known is that John Grubbs became John Burks.

With this simple act, my great-great grandfather once again entered the craft of teaching and leading, determined to share his gift of literacy. My grandfather, the ever-living Reverend Timothy M. Burks, concluded the family story by saying, "It's in your blood."

My grandfather reminded me that teaching and leading are parts of my heritage. He told me what my ancestor endured and what he accomplished. Surely, if Preachin' John could defy angry mobs, I could easily lead a school.

A few days later, I took a leap of faith and left the University School of Nashville to become the second principal of Crockett Elementary School.

YOUR REFLECTION

Mark Twain wrote, "Courage is not the absence of fear, it is acting in spite of it." How have you behaved courageously in the past? Where do you want to grow in courage and why? Describe the zaniest thing you have done that still brings a smile to your face. When have you taken a leap of faith? How are you different because of the experience? Who—from your past or present—has inspired you?

ONLY FLOWERS BLOOM SILENTLY

At the ripe old age of 27, I accepted my first principalship; since then my life hasn't been quite the same. One evening after a fairly long day at work, I reread an email message I'd sent to family and friends a few weeks after I began my first principalship.

dear all: last sunday sometime after church, i made my way to work. i'd initially planned to file away mounds of papers, but found myself being drawn to our grassy playground. i yielded to temptation and decided to take along my kite. now, you must understand i've not flown a kite since "dog was a pup". i placed my multicolored piece of therapeutic equipment on the ground; commenced to unravel a bit of string; and wondered seriously if i could write-off my kite on this year's taxes.

the southern winds were terrific and the sun was

beaming. in an instant my kite was airborne. things went well. the truth is, my mind began to "drift" once i got the kite up. it wasn't long before i began to compare leading a school (or any organization, for that matter) to flying a kite. you need more than favorable winds to keep a kite afloat. like the playground field where i flew my kite, my job comes with specific parameters. i—as a principal—and we—as a school family—can only go so far. once the kite's in the air, it [can] take on a life of its own. and what's more, when you think you're controlling it, you really aren't.

so, what keeps our high-flying friend in the air? of course, a good gust of air and string tension are essential. give the kite too much slack and it dips and drops. pull it too tight, the string snaps and you lose your whole enterprise. ahhh, but when it's really up there and the wind is to your back, no one sees you. folk only see what's really important. they see your kite flying and soaring—a thing to behold.

Two days after sending out this email message, Sterling H. Hudson III, the man who is largely responsible for my entrée into education responded to my "update." Dean Hudson wrote,

> Very interesting analogy. When I think of kite flying, I think of Charlie Brown whose kite always seems to end up in a dreaded tree. But you know what, Tony? Charlie Brown never hesitates to loft another kite even with the prospect that yet another tree might eat it. This is the epitome of perseverance. Stay encouraged. Remember, God's supply of kites (and trees to eat them) is unlimited.

And did I ever have an unlimited supply of kites and trees during my time as a new principal! I wasn't looking for a principalship and I could've easily stayed at the University School of Nashville teaching history and philosophy until retirement. Because of this, I had yet to take the state's required administrator licensing examination.

Before I started my first day on the job, an article about me appeared in the local newspaper, emblazoned above the fold:

> "Hiring of young principal prompts call for new policy".

> Tony Burks, 27, principal designate for Crockett Elementary School, is a history teacher at University School of Nashville and has served as headmaster for the summer session. But his youth and years of experience have one school board member saying the principal standards should be tougher.[5]

A photographer had even managed to snap a shot of me in the school cafeteria having a lunchtime conversation with kindergarteners as they queried me about becoming their new principal. Parents questioned my credentials and educational pedigree. A few even contacted the superintendent to ask why he'd hired a "n**ger principal" to lead a school that was 98% white.

The scrutiny didn't end there. Some parents were concerned about class assignments, others were concerned about new teachers, and still others were concerned about grading practices. Two veteran teachers challenged almost every classroom observation and evaluation I completed. Several

---

[5] Nancy Mueller, "Hiring of Young Principal Prompts for New Policy," *Tennessean*, December 10, 1998, first edition.

teachers packed their bags and transferred to work with their former principal.

We had three educators die in the span of 14 months. One student died tragically in a car crash with her mother. Many of my elementary school babies witnessed the play-by-play reporting of the tragedy on September 11, 2001.

Someone vandalized my reserved parking sign, scrawling vulgar language about me. A band of parents secretly met with the new superintendent to question my fitness for duty because two third-grade students plotted an escape from campus. I spent a full year with two central office administrators monitoring my every decision. And a special educator falsely accused me of sexual harassment. She said I'd invited her to spend the night with me in a hotel. A lot of learning and leading was compressed into 3½ years.

For every negative experience, I encountered students who were appreciative of my ability to connect with them and observe them as learners and leaders. Because of my students, I honed my craft of telling and reading stories (what I now call "storyWeaving") through weekly All School assemblies. I vividly remember Alexandria Peyton Kennedy, a precious little kindergartener, wondering aloud within earshot of me if it was permissible for her to like the former "girl principal" and me, the new "boy principal" at the same time. I assured her she wouldn't betray Dr. G. by liking me as her new principal.

For every negative experience, I built strong relationships with staff—from the custodian and the main office team to the classroom teachers and the school counselor. I remember welcoming a veteran educator who had been mistreated by her principal. She was crestfallen and apprehensive in the aftermath of her experiences. She joined our team and I invited her to give our students her very best. She took the yearbook home that night and mastered the names of every student in the school! I remember two teachers—they dubbed themselves "The Bookends" because they taught the same grade level and came as a set—who took me under their wings and exposed me to teaching at its best. They reminded me that classrooms should gush with healthy noise because "only flowers bloom silently."

And now, many years later, I reflect on those times and the lessons learned. Even now, I often travel with a kite. Whether in a city park after a day of work or on an island for vacation, I still find kite-flying to be a meditative experience. The twists, surges, and turns my kite makes as it encounters the ever-changing wind invites a deeper reflection on lessons learned. It is so important to seek out and embrace the challenges of life. It is through them that we develop as individuals.

YOUR REFLECTION

Kites symbolize freedom and joy. Think about your life: What are the joys (or kites) you've experienced? What are some challenges (or trees) in your life? How have you overcome your challenges? What makes you soar like a kite? What is preventing you from experiencing joy?

A PLACE AT THE TABLE

Whenever I am asked to speak about my experience starting a school from scratch, I think of my students and students like Amir.[6] Amir left an established high school that had more than a century of history as an academic and athletic powerhouse to enroll in a fledgling early college high school that had neither athletic teams nor a proven record as a school. Amir was at a disadvantage for admission to The Early College at Guilford (ECG) by the intersectionality of race, gender, and socioeconomics. The perceptions of some of the parents and guardians of identified gifted and talented students, the perceptions of one of my immediate supervisors, and perhaps the perceptions of some students at ECG were that

---

[6] This story of Amir—a composite of two students of color who attended The Early College at Guilford—explores a series of culturally courageous decisions I made as a principal.

Amir—and students like him—had no place at a school established for high-achieving gifted students. I wrestled with the decision to accept his application for admission. As one of the first early college high schools in the nation, we were "designing, building, and flying the plane" all at once and were developing protocols and procedures along the way. I embraced a moral commitment to educational access, equity, and excellence, and then I admitted Amir.

Through the decision to admit Amir, and other decisions like this, I embraced the notion of transformative leadership espoused by Astin and Astin and the hope they have for its widespread use:

> *We believe that the value ends of leadership should be to enhance equity, social justice, and the quality of life; to expand access and opportunity; to encourage respect for difference and diversity; to strengthen democracy, civic life, and civic responsibility; and to promote cultural enrichment, creative expression, intellectual honesty, the advancement of knowledge, and personal freedom coupled with social responsibility.*[7]

[7] Alexander W. Astin and Helen S. Astin, Leadership Reconsidered: Engaging Higher Education in Social Change (Battle Creek, MI: W. K. Kellogg Foundation, 2000), 11.

In retrospect, my decision to admit Amir was an effort on my part to "expand access and opportunity." The national, state, and local emphasis on rigor, relevance, relationships, and results is designed to advance the basic principle of equity, which posits that the greatest inequity is to treat unequals equally.

School reputations and demographics are wedded in today's age of accountability, and in this race to the top mindset, some educators would rather protect schools from students whose test scores might lower a school's overall performance. The politics of equity suggest that when educators know a school's test score results, they can predict with great accuracy the demographics of the school. If this is plausible, then the reverse is equally feasible: if a person is told the race and socioeconomic status of students, that person can predict the students' achievement and performance on standardized tests. Schools populated by those on the "right side" of everything tend to have funding that equitably supports rigor. Those on the other side—often students of color—are more likely to attend schools that have lower per-student funding which results in less support for teaching and learning.

The Early College at Guilford could have easily been exclusively populated by students who were white, wealthy, and advantaged. This necessitated that we as an admissions team maintain a moral commitment to equity. Our equity work did not stop at the end of the admissions process. I chose to be courageous and resist the ongoing question posed by naysayers along the way: "Could Amir handle it?" When rigor and equity are part of a solid education all students are intellectually (and appropriately) stretched.

Amir was challenged beyond measure by interactions with high school peers, college classmates, and professors. I knew whatever I designed for Amir would benefit all students. We met with each grade level weekly to nurture and grow school culture and climate. Students led assemblies and taught fellow students during four-to six-week-long mini-courses on everything from the use of scientific calculators and cooking with a microwave to public speaking and knitting (yes, knitting). We introduced students to the "office" hours concept and empowered them to meet with their teachers about coursework.

Students took ownership of their learning and radically shifted the pendulum from "getting" grades to "earning grades." The goal was to achieve mastery of a subject all while exploring a diversity of opinions, ideas, and beliefs. For students who struggled to experience success, we reviewed their overall performance each quarter and held Student-Centered Success Conferences with students and their families to generate processes and protocols to ensure students were achieving academically and socially. We didn't start out with this concept in place. We soon learned a hard lesson; from then on, we had key supports in place to support each student.

Our students established over 25 clubs and organizations—a testament to the 150 students enrolled at the school at the time and their commitment to creating spaces to welcome all. Over time, even the notion of teaching and learning evolved to be student-centered and hands-on in support of all students.

Because of his experiences at our school, wherever Amir ventured, educators and peers alike recognized and respected his pioneering nature, convivial spirit, and dedication to academic and social excellence. And for these traits I am proud to call Amir one of my shining stars.

YOUR REFLECTION

Describe a time when you made a decision that was unpopular. What personal principle or philosophy guided you in reaching your decision? What was the impact of your decision? It has been said that hindsight is 20/20. As you reflect on your decision, what made it wise in hindsight? If you were faced with the same circumstances, how might your decision be different now and why?

WALK WITH PRINCESSES

If you can talk with crowds and keep your virtue,
Or walk with kings—nor lose the common touch,
. . . .
Yours is the Earth and everything that's in it
"If" by Rudyard Kipling

Once in a while, we happen to be in the right
place at the right time. Such was the case the
summer of 2006 when I travelled to Thailand on a
six-week Fulbright Administrator Exchange. The
Administrator Exchange was one of several
signature Fulbright programs between the United
States of America and the Kingdom of Thailand. I
was the sole American selected to participate in the
Administrator Exchange with Thailand that
summer. I was paired with Sali Kasemrat who'd
served as the principal of a bustling school in
Chachoengsao due east of Bangkok. Sali is a strong
and graceful senior educational leader and a

powerful advocate for cross-cultural learning and international exchanges.

My arrival coincided with the 60th Anniversary of His Majesty The King, Rama IX of Thailand's ascension to the throne. I wanted to be a good guest so I took dozens of items to give away as gifts, including several copies of an anthology of student poetry. Sali took me all over the country to meet people and learn about Thai culture. Most days we learned about the Royal Family and I soon recognized the colors associated with each (the King was born on a Monday so his color is yellow).

We knew that Her Royal Highness, The Princess Maha Chakri Sirindhorn of the Kingdom of Thailand, was visiting my exchange partner's province because her royal cypher and flags were visible everywhere along the countryside. My exchange partner had previously told me of Her Highness's love of poetry and suggested that I give her a copy of the anthology of student works. "Yeah, right," I said in my "whateva" voice, "Not in a million years will they let me, a country boy from Alabama present something to the Crown Princess." I thought about her security team (they're quite smile-free in the "Land of Smiles") and my command of basic Thai (it's so horrible that my exchange partner once asked, "what language are you speaking?"). Then I remembered a storied poem of Kipling called *If.* I'd memorized it while pledging Alpha Phi Alpha Fraternity, Incorporated, in similar fashion as my elder brothers had done, including Marc Fields, Christopher Jolley, and the Reverend Doctor Martin Luther King, Jr.

To make a short story long, my exchange partner, Sali, was well-connected in the Thai educational community and well-versed in Thai protocol. I was able to give the Princess the book of poetry. I was sent to the school's library where I was eventually introduced to Her Highness as an "American Fulbrighter" who had something to present. I bowed and lifted the pedestal holding the book. Much to our surprise, the Princess didn't just take the book and move on; she asked a few questions about the poetry and then inquired about my experiences with the Fulbright Administrator Exchange. Over the following weeks, I shared the remaining books of poetry with Thai people from all walks of life, and they were equally impressed with our local public library's efforts to inspire a new generation of poets.

In 2010 I returned to the Kingdom of Thailand to celebrate the 60th Anniversary of the Fulbright Program in the country. Her Royal Highness, the Princess of the Kingdom of Thailand, was the

Keynote Speaker, and somehow out of hundreds of Fulbrighters in attendance, I was asked to stand in the Exhibition Area as the Princess viewed the displays. I'd packed one copy of the subsequent book of student poetry and held it aloft as she strolled by my station. She did a triple-take, approached me, and struck up a conversation as if we'd spoken to each other just yesterday.

After returning home from the Fulbright Administrator Exchange, I reminded our student poets of Dr. King's words, "If a man is called to be a street sweeper, he should sweep streets even as Michelangelo painted, or Beethoven composed music, or Shakespeare wrote poetry. He should sweep streets so well that all the hosts of heaven and earth will pause to say, 'Here lived a great street sweeper who did his job well.'" It wasn't that she recognized or remembered me. What mattered was that she remembered the work of my young poets. You never know who will see your work. You never know the impact of what you say or do. You never know the reach of your legacy.

YOUR REFLECTION

What is your passion? What do you do well? You
never know who will see your work; how do you
ensure that what you create is an excellent
masterpiece?

BELIEVE

Many years ago, Frank Marshall Davis charted the story of "Roosevelt Smith" in a poem of the same name. Davis wrote,

You ask what happened to Roosevelt Smith
Well…
Conscience and the critics got him
Roosevelt Smith was the only dusky child born and bred
in the village of Pine City, Nebraska.
At college they worshipped the novelty of a black poet
and predicted fame [8]

Roosevelt Smith had what my great-grandma Nettie would call "a hard row to hoe." From age 23 to 31 Roosevelt Smith published five books

---

[8] Frank Marshall Davis, "Roosevelt Smith," in John Edgar Tidwell, ed., *Black moods: Collected poems* (University of Illinois, 2002), 52.

reflecting the spectrum of human experience and exploring distinct forms and styles. Each time he devoted a few years to working and observing, striving for a different medium of expression. And each time Roosevelt Smith was met with zingers from his writing critics. When the reviews about his final book were released, Roosevelt Smith put down his pen and paper at the ripe old age of 31. He stopped writing forever. In the years since I first discovered this poem, I've had to remind myself who I am and *whose* I am.

My mentor superintendent encouraged me to spread my wings and soar into my own superintendency. "He's right," I thought as I explored opportunities around the country. I ultimately pursued two superintendent positions in the Deep South. In May 2011 I was one of five finalists for service as superintendent of my hometown school district. Then on June 30, 2011, after three years of service, I was laid off as a Regional Superintendent from one of the largest public school districts in the nation. My colleagues and I were financial (and political) casualties of the state's worst economic crisis in a generation. I went from earning a salary of $155,000 a year with budgetary oversight for about $122 million to receiving $425 a week in unemployment and living in the guestroom at the home of a principal I once supervised. Within hours of me getting a layoff notice, Maude Patrick offered me a place to live. "Dr. Burks, you're welcomed stay with my family until you sort things out." I assured Maude I'd addressed everything and had settled on my lodging. About two weeks later she contacted me, "You know you're welcomed to stay with us, Dr. Burks." She was direct the third time, "Tony, it just doesn't make sense to spend that much money on a studio apartment when you can stay with our family rent free until you find a position that works for you." I moved in within the week.

Shortly afterward, I was one of six—and then one of two—finalists to become the next superintendent of another small school district. I didn't get the position and for the first time in my career I questioned my God-given talents. As I explored career opportunities in California, Alabama, and Georgia that year, I moved from situations where senior leaders "had my back" as advocates and believed in my capabilities to positions where my passion and practices were questioned.

After nearly a year of searching, I'd finally been recruited as an assistant superintendent at another large school district. I would soon discover that personal vendettas and political motives would result in petty abuses of power.

I had been granted personal leave for several days to attend the second inauguration of President Barack Hussein Obama with my family and friends, but was still leery of missing the monthly school administrator meetings. I'd driven all night, grabbed an outfit, and arrived at the monthly meeting about 30 minutes before the principals I supervised. Relieved, I conversed with my colleagues in the atrium of the auditorium as we awaited the start of the meeting. Just then, the Deputy Superintendent's assistant approached me and ordered me to return home to change into professional attire. She made this directive in the proximity of a half dozen of my colleagues. I was mortified.

I happened to be wearing a Black Guess turtleneck sweater, a pair of black Kenneth Cole boots, and a pair of gray Brooks Brothers dress slacks; an outfit I'd worn many times before.

Confused and humiliated, I made the 50-minute round trip drive to change. A week later in the face-to-face meeting I demanded, my supervisor asked, "Are you aware of the board policy on acceptable dress?" I told her I was very well aware of the policy as I had read the entire board policy manual from cover-to-cover, not two months before. I knew I was safe.

She told me I was sent home for wearing "other attire as deemed inappropriate by the supervisor." She relied on the fine print of a broadly worded policy that encompassed attire from suits for classroom teachers to sweats for coaches and physical education teachers to justify sending me home at her discretion. That was the beginning of the end of my tenure in that role and my service to the district.

I have been an educator for nearly 25 years. Not once had I been sent home for inappropriate clothing. In fact, my keen fashion sense, my tailored suits, trademark bow-ties, and colorful eyewear have been an enduring signature of mine. It was only in this district, one where I was working differently and actively building strong connections with my team and those I supervised did things like my eyewear and clothing become issues.

There is no testimony without tests. In the months after the layoff, I had multiple opportunities to be like Roosevelt Smith, to buy into the madness, to host a pity party by sending a special invitation only to myself. In my darkest hour my grandfather whispered from his grave, "It's in your blood. Hold your head high. Stick your chest out. You've got a strong name that your great-great-granddaddy, Preachin' John, chose purposefully." The incessant questioning of my decisions and integrity and regular attempts to belittle and minimize my accomplishments and professionalism remain unwarranted years later. If I hadn't drawn on my heritage, this experience would have crushed me.

I've been able to grow and learn in places around the country. I've reflected on my tenure in various districts and discovered a few commonalities. Advocates are invaluable, especially those culturally courageous leaders who are not afraid to walk the talk. For four years I served as Superintendent-in-Residence with the National Center for Urban School Transformation at San Diego State University. I know that this role is a mouthful to say. Basically, I worked with some of the lowest performing schools across the country. I supported principals in "transforming" what they do with and for schools so that their students graduate capable of entering college or the world of work. I was among five educators highlighted in *Walking the Equity Talk: A Guide for Culturally Courageous Leadership in School Communities.* I conquered a fear of public performance, studied ballet for one year, and performed before an audience of 1,000. I began studies at a school of ministry. I was featured as one of "six HBCU graduates to know" in *NU Tribe Magazine*. I relaunched my consulting practice where I now serve as Chief Learning Officer coaching and training leaders for excellence. I have also spent time with family and living life without regrets.

I have encouraged my protégés to reflect on their journeys, serve their communities, and support their own protégés and others coming behind them. Together we are conquering fears, celebrating accomplishments, and launching personal and professional endeavors. Each day presents new opportunities for us to refuse to accept someone else's definition of who we are!

YOUR REFLECTION

Describe a time when you held a "pity party."
How do you hold your head high and keep the
faith when faced with critics? How might
comments from critics spur you on to greatness?
What did you discover about yourself through this
experience? How are you encouraging and inspiring
others?

GOING THE EXTRA MILE

I remember one time when I'd interviewed for a position. I'd made it through a paper screening. I'd completed a full battery of interviews and follow-up questions. Despite this, the State Department of Education still hadn't hired me as a School Turnaround Coach. I wanted this position so I could make a difference by partnering with underperforming schools to transform the educational outcomes of students. I was especially interested in the position because it complemented my work as Superintendent-in- Residence with the National Center for Urban School Transformation.

Perseverance, at times, is easier said than done. I'd done everything I was to do and there I was waiting and wondering and waiting and wondering. I figured the hold-up was in processing my "paperwork." I vividly reflected on my tenure months before as a regional superintendent.

I remembered the behind the scenes workings of the district's Human Resources division. I knew what I was like when I processed things to hire principals for my cohort. I knew that it would be equally—if not more—challenging to process my paperwork through a state department of education.

I didn't want to be a pest, yet I knew maintaining communication was essential. I wrote the contact person for the position and learned I'd impressed the team with my career experiences and my interview responses. They were considering the proper "fit" for me. I knew then I had to go the extra mile to close the deal.

As it were, I'd planned a post-holiday vacation in a neighboring state. I emailed the contact person and informed him I would be vacationing nearby. I told him I'd welcome the opportunity to drop by the state office to meet members of the team. I knew this would be another chance to interview with them. Little did they know I'd driven four hours that morning. I'd changed clothes in the car while parked adjacent to a coffeehouse. I suited up for the chance encounter and I'd even tied one of my trademark bow ties without the aid of a mirror. I arrived a few minutes early and conversed with the receptionist. One by one, I met team members as they returned from lunch; but, my time with the Division Head was limited due to a critical meeting called by the state superintendent.

Thankfully, I'd learned years ago to have my "elevator speech" ready to go and I delivered it to them in less than two minutes. I walked out feeling confident only to discover my rental car wouldn't start. I thought "This is a good omen! They don't want me to leave the building!" I learned that my future colleagues liked my instant rapport with everyone I met that afternoon. Furthermore, they were impressed I'd taken the initiative to arrange an impromptu meeting with them. Soon afterward I was informed that the Division Head had authorized my employment as a School Turnaround Coach. I'd gone the extra mile, and it had paid off.

The story didn't end there. Almost a month after the meeting, I still didn't have a contract or any sign that I would soon be employed. I came close to giving up on the opportunity; then I remembered I needed to persevere and go the extra mile to achieve the results I desired. I sent an electronic message to the contact person informing him of my continued interest in the School Turnaround Coach position. He replied and thanked me, saying things were still in the works.

A few weeks later, I was in the state on personal business. I was standing knee deep in mounds of artwork, furniture, and paperwork when my cellular phone rang. "Dr. Burks, I have your salary offer paperwork now and I'd like to fax it to you for your signature." I knew I needed to go the extra mile and I didn't miss a beat. "You won't believe it, but I'm in the state moving things into storage. I'm less than 40 minutes away from your office and if the team is willing to overlook how I'm dressed, I'll drive over and sign the document in person." Needless to say, when I arrived minutes later, I shocked them. I lived in San Diego, over 2,500 miles away from the office!

In this age of permanent whitewater, when things are constantly shifting, it is imperative that those who are interested in leadership positions persevere and go beyond the typical and everyday effort. Go the extra mile.

YOUR REFLECTION

What does perseverance mean to you? Describe a time when you persevered or were stretched. What helped you to "stick-with-it"? Who helped you along the way? What skills and traits did you develop (or hone) as a result of stretching? What are you experiencing now that could benefit from you "going the extra mile"? How are you persisting?

TRUTH BE TOLD

Someone asked me not long ago if I missed being an elementary school principal. Without missing a beat, I said, "Yeah, I miss the hugs. Kindergarteners have a special way of grabbing you about the knees. I miss seeing budding Jacob Lawrences, Shanequa Gays, I.M. Peis, and Georgia O'Keeffes dashing into my office to show me their latest works. I miss seeing a child finally grasp the skill of reading; but what I miss most of all is story time."

One day while going through "story time" withdrawal, I combed through my collection of books and selected an award-winning classic, *Click, Clack, Moo: Cows That Type* by Doreen Cronin.[9] (I get my fix by storyWeaving for children and adults at schools and in libraries. I often describe storyWeaving as a decidedly delicious blend of

---

[9] Doreen Cronin, *Click, Clack, Moo: Cows That Type* (New York, NY: Simon & Schuster, 2000).

telling and reading stories.) Then I made my way over to an elementary school to share a story with a large group I even brought along an old straw hat to role play!

Click, Clack, Moo is the story of Farmer Brown and his cows. Once the cows discovered a typewriter in the barn, they began sharing their concerns with Farmer Brown. The old barn was a touch drafty so the cows requested electric blankets to provide the comfort and warmth they desired. The farmer was put off at first by what the cows sought. Over time and with the assistance of other animals, however, he displayed his concern for them and met their needs. And peace was restored to the farm!

For whatever reason—maybe it was the story itself, or the day, or what I had for lunch—it made me think of the importance of communication. I thought of honest dialogue, the kind that sustains learning communities.

I remembered the "Status Checks" I'd conducted at The Early College at Guilford. I periodically gave our students graphic organizers to capture their opinions about what was working well and what needed our focus. What most folk don't know is that once I collected their comments, I shared them—the good, the bad, and the ugly—

with our faculty and staff. Students welcomed the challenge and choice of attending a public high school on the campus of Guilford College, a private institution. They enjoyed experiencing a diversity of opinions, ideas, and beliefs. Some students complained about the absence of lockers and traditional sports. Most loved the cafeteria food—a rarity among high schoolers. A few bristled at the frenetic pace of some of their courses or the delivery styles of some of their teachers and professors. For some staffers, it was painful. It was refreshing for others. For me, although it stung at times, it felt good knowing what we were doing well and the areas that warranted growth.

The story of Farmer Brown is illustrative because it cuts to the core: we achieve much more when we communicate and work together. The cows had a concern of importance to bovine. They didn't rely on Farmer Brown's non-existent mindreading abilities. They rallied together and made their issues known to the one who could address their needs (i.e., Farmer Brown). The cows put their concerns in writing and signed their names ("Sincerely, The Cows"). Also, they creatively enlisted the support of others to reach their goal (i.e., the chickens and a duck).

The great thing about environments that nurture communication is that we risk learning about our strengths, weaknesses, triggers, blind spots, and gifts in a world where many leaders are taught they must be perfect. It felt pretty good working in a place where most adults "told it like it is." We used protocols and structures to support our forward movement. Sometimes I'd begin a meeting by prompting participants to express their individual fear and hopes.

While we learned much about each other, a deeper purpose of using the Fears and Hopes protocol was to get potentially festering concerns out in the open so we might address them together. Like the time when a group of parents were distressed about the quality of the college recommendation letters their students were getting from our school counselor. I had the opportunity to review the letters, coach the staff member, and provide professional learning to staff and parents on the art of telling our students' stories through letters of recommendation. An initially strained moment became productive and mutually beneficial for all.

At other times I connected with our natural ability to make meaning through storytelling. I'd invite everyone to share insights about their own teaching and learning as a way to inform and direct our next steps organizationally.

Even with my vulnerability and openness as a leader, I'd get the occasional anonymous "A Concerned Parent" letter or the "it-has-come-to-my- attention" phone call about an issue. Like the time a parent complained to the Board of Education about my students walking out of their college-level classes to protest an ongoing war. Or when the superintendent contacted me after a few parents called the district office to complain about students choosing to wear graduation robes of different colors. Sometimes when things happened on campus, I was one of the last to know.

For the most part, however, parents and guardians were comfortable scheduling an appointment, sending an email, or just dropping in to see me. They were comfortable joining in and working towards a solution. They risked putting a face to their concerns, and they did this knowing the power of T.E.A.M.—"together everyone achieves more." Likewise, faculty and staff learned that I preferred "straight talk" any day.

More than anything, I felt comfortable sharing my thoughts candidly and respectfully with our school family, my supervisor, our superintendent, our school board, and the community at large. I learned to communicate authentically in ways that resonated. The power of *Click, Clack, Moo* and other stories is that, in their telling, listeners and readers are invited to become participants and shapers of what they hear and read. Stories often impart multiple meanings and truths because of this vital relationship. The storytelling power of a children's book allows us to embrace a truth or a keen insight and apply it to our lives. Truth be told, stories—as interactive bibliotherapy—enable us to take a closer look at ourselves and make a change for the better.

YOUR REFLECTION

Describe yourself as a communicator. What are your communication strengths? Where do you need to grow as a communicator? What is most challenging about communicating at home with family? What is most challenging about communicating at work? What is most challenging about communicating at leisure with colleagues and friends? How have you changed as a communicator? How does your "at home" communication compare to your "at work" communication?

BYSTANDING

Because human [beings are] endowed with empathy,
[we] violate the natural order if [we do] not reach out to
those who need care.

\- Saraswati

"Stay in your lane; mind your business," is what I said to myself and I focused on the phone call. "How are you this evening, Debbie? I'd like to request a shuttle . . ." I looked around just as a little girl on an escalator lost her grip on the handrail.

"Stay in your lane; mind your business. Remember you are the sole black man in this baggage claim area. She's a little white girl. This is America. You're in Connecticut. People have guns. They shoot first and ask questions later. Folks don't always respond positively to Black men running . . . even if it's to help. Even if you're a 'good guy.' Even if you're a doctor (not the hospital kind 'who can cut people up,' but a doctor nonetheless)."

"Stay in your lane; get to your rental car, and to your awaiting hotel room. Plus others are closer; they'll step in." "Sir? Sir? Are you at the terminal?" the voice on the other end of the line asked.

I looked around, no parent in sight, and did what good people do. I dropped the phone, ran towards the child, scooped her up, and rode the escalator up to where I prayed her parents would be.

Onlookers focused on her parents to see their reaction to a wailing little white girl safely cocooned in the arms of a tall, bespectacled Black man. I waited, too. This is America. People have guns. They shoot first and ask questions later.

The mother crouched to hug her daughter, and she gently whisked the hair from the child's face. The father never lost eye contact with me. His face betrayed him; he was conflicted. They hadn't realized they'd left one of their two children near the lower level baggage claim area. She'd been understandably mesmerized by the syncopation of the whirring escalator. The father was understandably mesmerized by me.

"Thank you, thank you," cried his wife. "No problem . . . I used to be a school principal . . . it's what we do." I turned around and descended the escalator as my heart drummed.

I spent the bulk of the shuttle ride to the rental car agency analyzing my response to the situation: "Why did I hesitate before responding? What does that say about me as a human being? What does that say about the current climate in the United States of America?" I zipped through the line at the rental car agency. I really wanted to share my experience with someone. I scanned the room: we were an eclectic mix of travel-weary people, so I kept my story to myself.

On the long drive to the hotel I replayed the scene and asked more questions: "Did I hesitate because of fear?" *Yep.* "Was I worried about being mistaken for a threat?" *Absolutely!* "Did I respond out of love?" *Ultimately—luckily for her—I did not stay in my lane. I acted. I led with love and not with fear.* "What if I had taken a second longer?" *I didn't, so I don't even want to consider the possibilities of inaction.* "What if the child had been injured as I watched as a bystander?" *I wouldn't have forgiven myself.* "What if she had been a child of mine?" *I would have wanted someone to get involved.*

My responses to most of the questions speak as much to my concern with my well-being as a Black man in the United States as they do to the notion of people staying in their lanes and minding their own business. We are in the space where people are emboldened to take life-ending action before asking a single question of clarity. I did wonder for a moment if I was putting my life in jeopardy to save a child from being harmed by a rapidly moving escalator. This is America. People have guns. They shoot first and ask questions later.

YOUR REFLECTION

Think about three moments in your life: one where you were a victim of something, one where you were a bystander (who did nothing), and one where you were an upstander (who did something). What might you lose by being a bystander in a situation? What might you gain as an upstander? How might your life be if you followed the words of American writer Og Mandino who offered, "Beginning today, treat everyone you meet as if they were going to be dead by midnight. Extend to them all the care, kindness, and understanding you can muster, and do it with no thought of any reward"?

SPEAK HIS NAME

There is an African Proverb that says, "as long as you speak his name, he shall live forever." When I got the phone call that Wednesday, I decided that father/mother God must've needed a gourmet chef or a truth talker, so God called my friend, Trover Reeves; God called Peanut. If we had been in control of things, I am sure things would have worked out differently. We would have held on to Trover just a little while longer. But God was in control and I could see my friend saying:

I have only just a minute,
only sixty seconds in it,
forced upon me can't refuse it
didn't seek it didn't choose it,
I must suffer if I abuse it,
give account if I lose it,
just a tiny little minute,
but eternity is in it.

Trover's minute lasted 35 years; and, when it was time, God called Trover to eternal rest. It is no coincidence that Trover transitioned from this earthplane during the time we recognize as Jesus' 40 days in the wilderness. Time Jesus spent pondering his purpose in life.

Trover and I were members of the Keystone Club at Hawk-Houston Boys Club in my hometown in Alabama. Over the years, our club traveled across the country to Keystone Annual Conferences learning powerful lessons—lessons that would shape our lives, lessons that would chart our paths.

At the Chicago Keystone Conference we met the "hawk," that infamous wind known for chilling you to the bone. We loaded in Slim's van and plowed through the snow and arrived at a winter wonderland. Southeast Alabama hadn't prepared us for that kind of weather. We were a mighty band of black boys trudging through the slush and feeling the hawk nibbling at our ears and toes and noses. It took a visit by a local television personality to warm our hearts and minds. We met Oprah Winfrey. Before she was just Oprah or just O. Before the *Color Purple* and *Beloved*. Before the book club and Dr. Phil. Or as Mike Jones would say … *That* Oprah, you know "Back then they

didn't want her, now she's hot they all on her."
Oprah Winfrey encouraged us to make a difference
and change the world one day at a time.

They say things are bigger in Texas and Dallas
didn't disappoint us the year it hosted the Keystone
Conference. Rev. Delbert Bradley, the Program
Director at the club, carted us down to the Lone
Star State where we came face to face with reality:
Texas opened our eyes to cultures beyond our own.
Sure, we witnessed the Texas of Jock and Sue Ellen
and JR characters on television's *Dallas*. But Texas
was more than that. Texas was about "black
cowboys" and the famed Buffalo Soldiers. Imagine
how it made us feel to know just a little more about
our history. Some lessons you never forget.

The Atlanta Keystone conference literally took
us to another level. One night we crammed into a
glass elevator and went to the tip-top of the Westin
Peachtree Hotel to have dessert. Imagine a cadre
of black boys from the Baptist Bottom in the five-
star Sun Dial restaurant as it slowly revolved giving
us a panoramic view of the Atlanta skyline. The
lessons learned from that experience told us that we
had within us the ability to rise to any occasion and
meet any challenge. We learned that we had the
right to sit at any table, anywhere. And we learned
that we must take responsibility for making sure

that others can get a seat at the table. Dr. Kenneth Bynum, our advisor, helped us see it wasn't just about us, it was about others, too.

Trover and I—and friends like Kazuo, Keifer, Chester, Bob, Paul, Stevie, Craig, Cherokee, and Roddy—learned a lot from our time at the Boys Club (now Boys and Girls Club) in my hometown. The things we learned were carried with us to high school and beyond. When we felt we were being left out of important things about high school senior class, we advocated for inclusion, and when that didn't work, we started our own senior group to host our own events. From cookouts and parties to trips and meetings, Trover was in the middle of it all, making sure we got together, enjoyed ourselves, and relished our time together as if it were our last day on earth.

I was a nerd back then—some would say I still am—but it didn't matter to Trover. He was a friend through the years despite all of my quirks. When we were hanging out, I could just be me. It didn't matter that I couldn't dance or play tennis like he could. Trover didn't meet a stranger, while I was painfully shy and felt awkward and out of place in crowds. And that's really what it meant to be a friend of Trover's. Trover was real. He called it like he saw it—like my schoolmate Spanky. He—

like my classmate Inger and her fashions—dared to be different. He dared to be himself. He was comfortable in his skin. And he learned to love himself in a way that many us never will. I am thankful he was given life through his mother.

For all of the lessons we learned together at the Boys Club, none compare to the lessons he taught. Trover taught me to "*never be content with someone else's definition of me. Instead, define myself by my own beliefs, my own truths, my own understanding of who I am, [whose I am], and how I've come to be. And never be content until I am happy with the unique person I am.*"

YOUR REFLECTION

Recall a childhood friend who taught you lessons about life. What were those lessons? How have they shaped you and your journey? What lessons are you teaching others through your words and actions? How will you live forever through the lessons you are teaching?

AFTERWORD

What we need now are stories; stories of people. The truth is that more stories of living and learning need to be told today:

Stories of principle; principal stories.
Stories of the playground, the classroom, the library.

Stories of our schools, our homes, our faith communities, our courtrooms, our boardrooms.
Stories of the White House. Presidential stories.

Stories of courage, of death, of life.
Stories of faith, hope, and love. Teaching stories.

Stories of the setting sun and of the rising moon. Stories of triumph and challenge.

Stories of healing and renewal and wisdom.
Stories of the oneness and importance of all living things.

What's your story? Tell someone today. We're waiting.

SPEAKING AND CONSULTING

Dr. Tony Lamair Burks II facilitates writing retreats, hosts storyWeaving concerts, and leads workshops on various topics from relationships to succession planning to Vision Boards. He is available for speaking engagements, executive coaching, training, and corporate storytelling. For more information contact:

info@LEADrightToday.com
www.LEADrightToday.com
619-796-6463

ABOUT THE AUTHOR

Dr. Tony Lamair Burks II first learned the art and craft of public speaking and storytelling from his four grandparents in LA . . . Lower Alabama.

After graduating from Morehouse College with a philosophy degree, he began a career in education and reconnected with his passion for words. His stories— blending childhood experiences and educational issues—have appeared in newspapers in North Carolina and Tennessee and in books nationally.

A graduate of Trevecca Nazarene University and The University of North Carolina at Greensboro, he has been a featured StoryWeaver, workshop facilitator, and graduation speaker at dozens of public, private, and independent schools, public school districts, and universities in the United States and abroad. He is a Fulbrighter, a fellow of the British-American Project, and a New Thought School of Ministry student.

He is an award-winning education expert who helps individuals and organizations as a thought partner and executive coach. He was recognized by *NU·tribe Magazine* as one of *Six HBCU Grads You*

Should Know and was honored with the *Phaedra Parks S.O.S. Save Our Sons Award for Empowerment and Service.*

An avid reader and master whistler, he plans to open a holistic "bed and brunch" renewal center for artists, executives, and educators.

TCPI and Black Teacher Project in association with LEADright present

2017 LEADright Learning Cruise

July 10 - 15, 2017

Prices from $603 per person

Black Educators: Leveraging Who We Are to Teach and Lead for Equity

www.leadrighttoday.com/2017learningcruise

Itinerary for 5 Day Western Carribean Cruise

Mon Fort Lauderdale (Port Everglades), Florida
Tue *Workshops*
Wed Ocho Rios, Jamaica
Thu Grand Cayman, Cayman Islands
Fri *Workshops*
Sat Fort Lauderdale (Port Everglades), Florida

138

SUBMIT YOUR STORY!

Bought Wisdom, Volume II:
Only Flowers Bloom Silently

ABOUT THE BOOK

Bought Wisdom is the kind of wisdom you get from experiencing life and all it tosses your way. Inspired by *Bought Wisdom: Tales of Living and Learning* by Tony Lamair Burks II, *Bought Wisdom, Volume II* will be an interactive and reflective book of your stories. We intend to publish the book in fall/winter of 2018.

ABOUT YOUR STORIES

Bought Wisdom, Volume II: Only Flowers Bloom Silently shares real stories from real people. These are stories of resilience in the face of chaos, release when letting go is warranted, and restoration to move to the next level. Your stories may be personal and revealing, they may include drama and emotion, they may share what's horrible or terrific. Whatever the case, your stories are written from the heart and they teach us lessons you've learned from your triumphs and challenges. Go to www.leadrighttoday.com/SubmitYourStory to learn more and submit your stories.